The Taste of Words:
The Rainbow Moment
Written by: Meg Lynch

Becky,
No one I know
embodies this message
quite like you. Thank you
for being open + honest — it's
inspiring!

Meg

Copyright

Any words that are in quotations in this book are not my own words. While some quotations are broken up between poetry lines, all correct writers/authors/artists are located within the footnotes at the bottom of each page along with which piece of art these quotes were taken from or inspired by. For each chapter title page, the citation for the quote is located beneath the excerpt as: Band, "Song Title."

"How many kings stepped down from their thrones?
How many lords have abandoned their homes?
How many greats have become the least for me?
And how many gods have poured out their hearts
To romance a world that is torn all apart?
How many fathers gave up their sons for me?"

Downhere, "How Many Kings?"

Table of Contents

Acknowledgments

For my mother, who has been overwhelmingly inspiring through this season of our lives: Thank you so much for giving a new meaning to "His mercies are new every morning" by being the best role model I could ever look up to. Thank you for loving me through my anger and giving me grace every time I mess up. I will forever love you higher than the sky.

For everyone who helped me in the brainstorming process:
Anne Whitmore
Julia Putzke
Gina Viarruel
Chelsea Britt
Katie Patrick
Rhonda Carter
Sallie Johnson
Missy Kirkland
Nathan Lilly
J. Blair Sanders
Zach Winstead
Ellie Strickland
Sarah Denton
Brianna Mack
Caleb Jones
Jenny Jones
Shelby Marzen
Andrea Rogers
Jessica Rogers
Destiny Alewine
Tyler Vining
Megan Wehunt
Jordan Sanders
Delaney Burke

Matt Golden
Christie McGowan
Gordon Woodall
Andre Niklas
Cynthia Giles

For all the people who have supported me by sharing my work
without hesitation or prompting:
Madre Dearest
Marlene Sleevi
Reina Ortiz
Bri Mack
J. Blair Sanders
Sophia Sanford
Ashleigh Davenport

For my formatting go-to guru, Chris Holtsinger: Thank you
for always being available to the people who need your help.
You have saved many necks simply because you will say yes. In
a world that tells people to figure it out themselves solo, that
makes you incredibly valuable.

For Julia Putzke: I never would have made this happen without
you. Your fight and faith for others inspires me every single day.
You are the closest friend I will ever have, regardless of how
far we wind up from each other, and I am grateful to call you
bestie.

For Sarah Denton, who assisted me in poetry placement and
is overall a super encouraging friend: Thank you so much for
being a person I can always turn to. I can't wait to see where the
Lord takes your gentle heart.

For Cynthia Giles, who has never stopped believing in me once: Every poem you write and speak aloud is inspiring, even when people don't tell you it is. Your writing will reach many people; I know I don't have to tell you this, but don't you ever give up. Your talent is far beyond what you can measure.

For all the Hope*Writers and Glory Writers out there: Thank you for encouraging my heart and inspiring me to be all I can be and more. I am privileged to be part of these communities.

Lastly, and most importantly, this book is for God, the One Whom My Soul Loves, who has never let me go, not even when I have found myself most abominable: Thank You for giving me freedom with every breath I take and making this life worth living each and every moment.

Introduction

This book has finally happened! It took a lot of hard work to get here, but here we are, and what a beautiful place we find ourselves. This earth is not perfect, not by a long shot, but there will always be moments that lead us to joy and peace. Let this be one of them.

I want to talk about the meaning of the rainbow for a minute. Let me say first and foremost: the rainbow belonged to God before it belonged to *any* of us humans. Let us not forget His promise to remind Himself with every storm that He has chosen to be a good Father.[1] I also want to point out that the rainbow has many meanings to all sorts of different people. Of course, it stands for unity among the LGBTQ community, but did you know a rainbow baby is one born after the loss of a child? And when pets die, they go to the Rainbow Bridge to play with each other and wait for their owners.

In each of these cases, the rainbow is something people cling to for hope. It signifies a promise that whatever we are battling against will not last forever. The rainbow itself is a promise of God's continuing goodness throughout the ages, and it will always stand for this. People will continue to cling to the goodness of the rainbow promise, allowing its hope to bring them out of their hard circumstances. This is what the rainbow truly means. This is what this book is aiming to cultivate in the hearts of all who read it.

This volume gets its name from a poem I wrote a while ago. It portrayed a single moment, and it spoke right to my heart in the next few months as I felt my soul being lifted out of a deep, ugly pit and into a beautiful place filled with light and grace.

---

1 Genesis 8:20-22

1

There are tons of things I could say about The Rainbow Moment, but I don't think I should. I don't tend to be a person of few words, but I think I'll let the poem speak for itself.

The Rainbow Moment

Rogue ashes wisp away as burning
Embers guide the way,
Daring the prisoner to escape.

Over Death and Death's
Right hand,
Angels dance along the sand
Never leaving the bobbin
G skiff.
Everlasting is His name, they call.

Yahweh, its sound breathes
Eternal
Life.
Looking around the sunlit shore and stepping int
O the boat, his fleeing heart begins to soar.
Why have I been chosen? Angels

Grant him this chance;
Raising their wings in grand romance
Ever-seeking
Ever-searching the horizon for their
Next command.

"Beloved, we have come to help you.
Love has won.
Underneath your sadness, your woe, you know
Everything will be okay. You have been saved." He thought,

2

I must be dreaming.
Never would this happen to someone like me. He was
Depressed in his ways and
Indignant in his manners, but
Grace interceded.
Outward expressions of

Valiant gratitude
In the midst
Of insurmountable guilt – It was
Left at the wayside as
Every tear fell, and
The angels bore him heavenward.

During the year-and-a-half-long creation of this volume
of poetry, I went through several moments much like this one.
I found myself a prisoner of serious financial woe. I found
myself a slave to fear, then a slave to anger. I found myself
deep in pits of agony, with no conceivable way out, and I hid
myself from the light because of some deep-seated fear. In each
of these instances, I was hard-pressed to find myself a way out
of my misery…only, it's not up to us to find our own way, is it?

The original version of this poem had two sentences
attached at the bottom: "Rainbows are promises of all we can
be tomorrow in the face of all we were yesterday. Although our
stories are never the same, in this way, they are: His grace wins
every time." God had a fun time proving His goodness to me
throughout the long months of writing. He enjoyed watching
me start to believe again in what I've known my entire life:
I WILL change the world with my words, and He WILL be
faithful to provide all I need in every season of life.

Much like *The Everglow* by Mae, I intend for this book to
take you on an epic journey, or maybe several normal-sized

ones. Thank you so much for reading, for supporting me and loving my craft. I do hope this work of art will make a work of your heart. I know it will change your life because it changed mine. Please keep your heart open to change and your soul ready to soar.

Much love in Christ,
Meg

Red: I AM not Against You

"The shame that grips you now is crippling.
It breaks My heart to see you suffering.
'Cause I am for you; I am not against you…
If you could count the times I'd say, 'You are forgiven,'
It's more than the drops in the ocean."

Hawk Nelson, "Drops in the Ocean"

Come Back x3

There's a game my parents used to play with my brother and I in the pool or standing on the sidewalk when we were kids. I remember my mom taking my hands in hers gently. She'd give me this smile, and I knew it was time.

Three seconds' breath, then she'd push me.

"Go away; go away; go away."

She'd smile big and pull me close.

"Come back; come back; come back."

There was an ease to it, away and back, away and back, away and back, like swinging in the sea.

She always ended in the biggest bear hug I could imagine. She wouldn't let go until I promised to always come back.

This one time, mom had both me and my brother, each of us holding the others' hands, a circle.

"Go away; go away; go away."

"Come back; come back; come back."

And we all three pushed and pulled, the strength of us united making the game more intense than ever before. It almost took my breath away. I was afraid of going under water, that I'd drown.

But they never let me go, not even once.

And like any proper father, when we walk away from God, He calls us back.

We sing, "Let's go away; go away; go away."

His voice resounds, "Come back; come back; come back, My Darling."

He rejoices when we finally do.

And He never lets us go.

Chased After

When you don't think you are seen,
When the people around you act like you're invisible,
I see you.

When the depths of your unsearchable heart
Lie untouched by human hands
Or touched by them the wrong way,
I know your ache.

When all the world has turned away from you
And left you alone with all your pain,
I seek out your heart

When you feel unloved,
Unwanted, like garbage,
I send you little hints of all the ways I love you.

Like a good game of hide-and-seek,
I chase after you with gladness.

Trust

Trust looks like
> A welcoming smile that holds the door open for you on the
> worst day ever
> That certain look passing between friends that says it knows
> something is wrong but won't press you for details.
> A cloudless blue sky: "This is my world that I created to be
> enjoyed by you. Please treat her well."

Trust sounds like
> "I am here whenever you're ready."
> Silence, open and waiting patiently for vulnerability
> "Let Me love you. Let My love free you."

Trust feels like
> Being wrapped up inside a freshly washed-and-dried
> comforter at the end of long, hard day
> The warmth of a friend hovering close by not needing to
> know everything but willing to listen to it
> The rain that comes with peace and cleanses every part of
> your soul

Trust is
> Sacrifice for the ones you love
> Hope for the help that brings us out of our prisons
> A hug that never lets you go and lasts the whole day long

Trust is Christ in us.

God's Heart

You've probably heard:
There is a place in your heart only God can fill.

There's a hole each human is searching to fill,
And no amount of man-ufactured concrete can do the job
    right.

Only the Creator who chose your birth
Who numbered your days
And the amount of hairs on your head,
The One who carries every tear in a glass jar
Can create in you a clean heart,
Unblemished and unbroken,
Completely fulfilled.

Only the Son of Man who was sacrificed,
The pearl of greatest price,
Could ever lead you straight to Life in Freedom
Unchained by your Life of Old.

The Protector
The Healer
Will make you whole.

But here the poem turns,
See, it goes both ways.

The Father is ever pining for our love,
Sending out rays of His own.
They shine into the darkness,
Reaching into all the depths of the universe saying,
"Let me love you."

13

And, boy, does He love you.

And all the beauty of all the worlds are but a hint
Of all He longs to lavish upon each individual soul.
That sunset you fell in love with,
The might of the ocean's waves,
His Masterpiece work outmatches the rest—
His masterpiece of YOU

Step out in this knowledge:
"There's a place in God's heart only you can fill."[2]

---

2 My friend Chelsea Britt said this in an interview.

Oh, Sweet
First published in The Taste of Words: This is only the beginning 2014,
  2016

Oh, Sweet, this love for me, how can it be?
That He should think of me before my birth.
And in my mother's womb create purely,
A tiny, lovely thing, with so much worth.

Inside His faithful hand, His loving touch,
We find all life consumed in passion-fire.
He made us in His image, and, as such,
Created us to love and to inspire.

My God is for me; who can be against?
Though they be strong, My God is stronger yet.
I shall stand beside Him, my faith unfenced.
With Him on my side, I need never fret.

He grants me life with His every dear breath.
This Love is strong; this Love is true, to death.

To be the Perfect Love

To be the perfect love
The kind that remembers the names of every passing soul
To show people they are valued more than they know

To be the perfect love
The kind that prioritizes the desires of others, big and small
To make dreams come true in every place

To be the perfect love
The sacrificial lamb that makes all men free
To celebrate together one day forevermore

My Beloved

Darling Beloved,
First and foremost,
You are the focus of my affections.

Dearest Beloved,
Of all the Beloveds,
I am especially fond of you.[3]

Sweetheart Beloved,
I find contentment in being with you,
Now and forevermore.

Gorgeous Beloved,
Do you not see your beauty?
It outmatches the most perfect sunset.

Starlit Beloved,
With your sparkling eyes sending diamond light into the
universe,
Reach out to the world around you and show them my Love.

---

3   This poem was written before the movie *The Shack* came out, but it is a
direct quote, so I figured I'd let you know. ☺

Stitches
First published on meglynch203.wordpress.com: 7 December, 2016

Father, stitch Your hand in mine
Let us walk along the shores
Together
Grainy sands playing between our toes
Just You and me
Forever

Father, stitch my heart to Yours
Until my beating, beating, beating
Tunes in time to eternity's
Let Your rhythms become my own
And let Your love be the music my feet step in time to

Father, stitch our minds together, too
So that Your vision is my vision
Your thoughts my thoughts
Make Your purpose my purpose
And Your people my people

Father, stitch my life to Yours
I will take up my cross
And live to die each day
Together, we will be the light
And together, we will change the world
And together we will be
Forever

Showered in Peace

You start the day with
Hurricanes of condemnation and loathing.
With every step you take,
You fall deeper and deeper
Into the pit.

This destructive, destroying world
And all its helpless people
Have taught you to be ashamed
Of what you've done, said, thought,
Of who you are.

When you look around you,
When you see your environment,
All you see is shadows.
Darkness pervades the air.
Desperation invades your heart.

Something inside you sparks. *I have to get out of here.*
You gather all the energy you can muster,
And you run.
You leave the desolate behind
Heading for what, you do not know.

Up ahead, you see something new coming,
And you're fearful of the cloud bearing toward you.
You've left the terror-wind behind
For what?
To be caught up again in what you cannot control?

Cleansing waters now compete for your attention—
Showers of mercy and grace,[4]
But the weight of this rain is not oppressive.
A misting peace fills the air.
It lifts you, coaxes you, out of the dust.

You float easily with the rising tide.
Like the donkey stepping up with every shovel-full of dirt,
You can wile your way out of this mess.
But when you reach the top,
You find a smiling face full of love.

This giant looks down at you and says,
At last, I've found you.
His voice carries the tone of a thousand Valentine's hearts.
His smile awards your soul with the deepest kind of joy
You've never had the privilege of dreaming could ever exist.

And He tells you,
Let me bring you home,
Dear One.

And you answer,
Yes, Papa, please.

---

4 This line is a song by the band Jesus Culture.

His Love
First published in The Taste of Words: This is only the beginning 2014, 2016

His love sounds the same in every language.
It whispers in the darkness of the night
A song that only the souls of those desperate can hear:

You are Mine.
I am yours.
From now until the end.

Orange: You are Loved

He knew, before you ever took a breath,
There'd be days where you'd forget
How beautiful he made you.
But you are loved, oh,
Not because of what you've done, no.
Even when your heart has run the other way,
Nothing's gonna change his love.
And you are wanted,
Not because you are perfect.
I know that you don't think you're worth that kind of grace,
But look into his face; you'll know…"

Ellie Holcomb, "You Are Loved"

Ten things to know about you:

1. You would not be on this planet if you were not wanted.
2. You are a beautiful work of art, perfectly knit together by the Master Creator. He finds no flaws in you.
3. You were created for a purpose whether you realize it or not and whether you know what that purpose is or not.
4. You have nothing to fear. The One who owns the universe is watching over your every breath, every move, every moment.
5. You are never alone. The God who created all the heavens and all the earth never leaves your side.
6. You are not what you have done. You are not owned by guilt or shame. You can shed it like a little black dress and step into freedom in a single moment.
7. Your heart was made for grander things than the material possessions of this earth, things you cannot hold, but feel and know within your heart.
8. Your life is the sum of many moving parts, but like the pieces of a sandwich, you get to decide which parts stay and which parts go.
9. You have talents that, when mixed with the unique perspective and knowledge and experiences of your life, have never been seen before and will never be seen again.
10. You can change the world with God on your side. ALL things are possible.

All of this is true about you, the person reading these words right now. All of these good words are true about you.

Believe in Yourself

Bought with blood and loved
Even through the worst the
Land has to offer.
Inside your precious soul lies
Every solution you'll need to live.
Vehemently loved are you, through
Each circumstance you will find yourself. Trust

In who you are, and you will fade
Nevermore.

Yet in the darkness
Of the night, the fight,
Unfazed by your faith, evil will
Raise its ugly head.
So you will answer:
Even through the worst I have ever done, He has not
Left my side. Forgiveness is the
Foundation of my value, and so I wear the beauty of
    redemption.

Perpetual Priesthood
First published on meglynch203.wordpress.com: 21 February, 2017

Aaron, brother of Moses, spent much of his life after slavery being believed in by God.

Aaron isn't necessarily known for the good he did in the nation of Israel. Every preacher I've heard seems to hone in on the moment he loses faith. In Moses' absence, the people of Israel came to Aaron troubled about how long Moses had been gone. Doubt became the biggest player on the field, and Aaron allowed it to force his hand. He gathered the people's gold and made a statue of a young cow out of it, commanding the nation to bow to it in the name of God.

After Moses came down from the mountain to stop the idolatry Aaron had started, Aaron threw the blame on his people. Despite the fact that the golden calf was his own idea, Aaron tosses his people into the fire, and he goes so far as to say, "So they gave [the gold] to me, and I threw it into to the fire, and out came this calf."[5]

Really? It just came out that way?

That's not how that works, Aaron.

As my pastor said this Sunday, "You don't want a leader like that."

But despite the fact that Aaron almost got the nation of Israel swept out by God in a murderous rage,[6] he was still the human God chose to lead His nation into His goodness. Led by God's

---

5   This is verse Exodus 32:24 in the Holy Bible.
6   This story can be found in Exodus 32.

divine instruction, Moses anointed Aaron as Israel's first High Priest.

Regardless of that huge flaw in his character, regardless of the fact that Aaron deliberately led God's people astray – even as God was telling Moses about his promotion, God still gave Aaron this important task. God decided, "I know Aaron still has the potential to live into this position. I will still give it to him, forgive his misdeeds completely and fully, and trust him with this most holy work." God did not look into Aaron's actions. He looked into his heart and knew Aaron wanted to do good work and prove himself.

Aaron had allowed the people's doubt to make him forget what God had done for them; this promotion was God surrounding Aaron continually with His presence for the rest of his life so he would never forget it again. In Exodus 40:15, God orders Moses to admit Aaron and his sons into "Perpetual Priesthood." God gave Aaron and his sons – as a free gift – a forever job. Aaron would never lose his priesthood, and the generations of his sons and their sons would be secure in the temple, too. Not only did God look down and see the good in His child Aaron, He blessed him and his family for hundreds of years to come.

How's that for having God believe in you?

This is the Loving Father we have; despite our worst efforts and all our half-witted mistakes, God still sees the good in our hearts. God knows the beauty residing within us and chooses to look at that, no matter how ugly we feel or how bad we think we messed up.

When you don't think you're good enough, God knows you are. It really doesn't matter who you are or what you've done or said or thought. God loves you and wants to see you succeed. He will give you good gifts, new opportunities, when you least expect them.

You are Loved. Always.

Wake Up[7]

Wake up to the majesty that lives inside you.
If you show me a picture of the minutia of an atom
And a picture of the universe as a whole,
I can't tell the difference.
Did you know your mind is just as big and detailed and capable?

Wake up to the destiny hidden in your heart.
You've seen it before – maybe only in your wildest dreams.
That thing you long to do with your life – You can!
You've been gifted with talents beyond your imagination,
And the longer you practice the bigger and better they get.
Know that your dreams *can* come true.

Wake up to the beauty that defines who you are –
Even when you don't see it.
Royalty lives in your veins;
You live with a diamond-studded soul
Consumed in passion-fire.
Your beauty lies within your strength;
Nothing can withstand your fight,
But you can withstand anything that comes your way.

Wake up to the reality that you are loved.
The God of all the universe became human.
He lived a perfect life and died in your stead
So that you might live forevermore,
And He longs to lavish that same love upon you
So that in every moment, you will see –
And know – you are deeply, truly treasured.

---

7 This poem is inspired by the song "Wake Up" by All Sons and Daughters.

Wake up to these truths.
Wake up to life more abundant.

Be Who You Are

Be who you are
(Some self-love is way overdue)
And you will fly like a shooting star

Be proud of your scars
They are proof of the truth
Be who you are

Erase the bars
That have hindered your view
And you will fly like a shooting star

For He holds all your tears in a glass jar
Don't you know you are valued?
Be who you are

Know that you are
Loved through and through
And you will fly like a shooting star

When you're out near and far
Or standing in a Starbucks queue
Be who you are
And you will fly like a shooting star

Call Yourself

You are what you call yourself.
Torn
Worthless
Deserted

You are what you call yourself.
Complete
Valued
Part of the whole

You are what you call yourself
Loser
Faker
Heart breaker

You are what you call yourself
Friend
Winner
A New Creation

Call yourself whole
Call yourself new
Call yourself true

Call yourself that which is lovely, not nasty
Clothe yourself in the beautiful, not the ugly
Cling onto faith, not doubt
Call yourself free and honorable and good

Call yourself that which creates beauty
        You are not the destroyer of harmony
Say you add value when you walk into a room

33

Your presence does not devalue a thing
Speak out in courage and bravery
And fear will no longer hold you back
Believe you walk in splendor
And you will hang your head in shame no longer
Call yourself pure
For you have been made new

My Blood Type[8]

My blood type is H

Heavenly-made, Heaven-sent
My anatomy is perfection

Heart-melting happiness
Beating in time to
Love songs floating through the air

Helpful servant – that's me
Forever a fighter for those in need
For people too weary to help themselves

Healer of Wounds and Builder of Bridges
Destroying destruction with kindness and
Leaving rivers of love wherever I roam

A halo and wings I do not have
But that which I do is Yours

My blood type is I

Invited to live
With a spirit that will never die

Inspired to inspire
Created by a creator to create
Light in the darkness with a single Word

---

8   This poem is inspired by the "My blood type is coffee" sign at Grayson
Coffee House.

Impeccably impassioned
To run this course with joy
And make sure others can as well

Imbued with a soul
Intertwined with the strings
Of love and light

Inclusive of all
Exclusive to none

My blood type is S

Sure-footed and sure of mind
I was made to live this life

Secure in the steadfastness
Of the One who is able
Trust is my middle name

Strung pearls of solid gold
I bring to you
Because of His sure faithfulness

Sweet worship songs I sing
To Him, the only King
Leading others to do the same

Surpassing all mankind's expectations
On the wings of eagles

My blood type is H-I-S

Hope for all mankind lies
Instilled within my
Soul forevermore

My blood type is HIS

I Am

**This is an overrated form of poem used in high schools that I just really
love.*

I am a lover of all things sweet,
From Pooh Bear to ice cream,
From babies to buttons and bubbles,
My middle name is Sugar

I am, unapologetically, a dog owner.
My Annie saved my life in high school
And proved God's love to my weary soul.
My Maxy's fur is softer than your dog's,
And my Lily is vindictive but a sweetie at heart.

I yam who I yam…
I love laughing and joking and having fun.
Puns are the greatest form of rhetoric,
And I will believe that 'til the day I die.

I am an adventurer,
Curious by nature.
With questions upon questions,
I long to figure out the issues of life
Through reaching out, climbing, discovering,
But never jumping to conclusions.

I am a writer!
Words are my life –
The ways they fit together,
The ways they don't –
Are part of who I am at my core.

But I am so much more than this.

I am loved – through and through.
This love has engrained itself in every fiber of my being, so
there will be no doubt about it.
Even when I don't feel love, I know it's there holding me tightly,
securely
Because He never lets go.

I am enough.
My Creator made me to live this life.
Even when I don't feel like I can make it, I know I can
Because I wouldn't be here if we couldn't face this thing
together.

I am a Difference Maker.[9]
My closeness to my Father will allow me to change the nations.
Of that, I am sure.
Even when I feel invisible, I know the little things I do make a
difference for the people around me
Because our hearts are shaped by every living thing under the
sun, and all good things make an impact.

I AM is a title of the Most High God,
And I am honored to say I am His.

---

9   This concept comes from the song "Difference Maker," by NEED-
TOBREATHE. It's a good song. You should look it up. ☺

See Her

see her feet
they aren't very pretty
her toes are crooked and
calluses cover her soles
she's played in the grass and
stomped in puddles barefoot and
been to rocky places
she isn't afraid to go where no one's gone before

see her hips
watch her saunter
to the steady rhythm of her soul
study how she moves
silently, swiftly, truly
knowingly
like the eye of the storm
unaware of the effect she has
on all who draw near

see her shoulders
broad and strong
they carry loads not many others can
they lean back slightly
she walks in confidence
like a queen

see her smile
see the joy she shares
she knows who she is
and where she's going
she isn't afraid to bring others along for the ride

see her eyes
the light inside
glowing embers of all the world could be
her core guidance
her one driving force
awake and alive for all to see

see her
she is beautiful

He Wanted You

A spark in the heart of The One,
Life began.
"I will call her…Meg."

He smiled as He saw me
He heard my laugh for the first time
And watched me grow
A thousand times before I was born

He watched my imagination soar
As I discovered the written word and all it could entail
He joined me in Narnia and at Hogwarts
And felt my need to create my own
    – A place where people could find safety and hope

He watched as I jumped into the ocean
Spinning, twirling like a madwoman
And He delighted with me as I delighted in its depths
Aching to be swept away from the stress and hurry of my world

He watched me giggle at the circus and the zoo
Dance along with the marching band at football games
Sigh in contentment when I found my Peaceful Place
And He felt those things along with me
Even before they'd happened

And He saw all the bad I'd ever do

He watched me for Those Ten Months
He saw me break the hearts of my closest friends
And treat people Less Than in every single way
He saw me lash out in anger

At those least deserving
Then hesitate at the apology

He saw me lie and cheat and steal
Tear down and destroy
In every moment before my birth

He knew all this
All the hang-ups and bang-ups
Yet He created me
Yet He chose me

And He knows all of you.
Your hang-ups and bang-ups
And He has chosen you as well.

He took one look at my gnarled heart
And saw only beauty

It doesn't matter what you've done
Or where you've been
If you are here on this earth
He has chosen you
To be loved by Him

Yellow: Struck Down but not Destroyed

"I am pressed, but not crushed,
Persecuted, not abandoned.
Struck down, but not destroyed.
I am blessed beyond the curse,
For his promise will endure,
And His joy's gonna be my strength."

Darrell Evans, "Trading My Sorrows"
see also 2 Corinthians 4:7-10 (ESV)

There will be days

The world will cave in
Several times in your life.

It will fall apart at the seams,
And you'll sew it back
Just as much.

All the bad things
You never thought would happen
Will.

They will happen
When you least expect them.

They will tear your heart out
And stomp on it mercilessly

You will pick it back up
And keep going.

You will piece together the tatters
And start over again.

But there's one thing you should know:
Each time you put your heart back together,
It grows stronger.

Every time you pick up the pieces,
Every time you stand up again,
You become a new person.

The world might bring unthinkable heartbreak,
But you consist of unimaginable strength
Unquestionable stamina
Unbearable beauty.

There will be days when you want to give up,
But you keep fighting
You try to breathe, and you make it through
Because you're a survivor, and that's what you do.[10]

---

10   The last two lines of this poem have been edited from a one-liner in *The Taste of Words: This is only the beginning.* "I try to breathe, and I make it through because I'm a survivor, and that's what I do."

11/10/16

Red is the color of my raging heart
As all the hurt and anger of the past few days floods over.
    (It doesn't help that I haven't eaten much today.)

My friend Gina
Who takes such good care of all of us
Has been blindsided by the biggest FEAR bomb the devil has
    to throw
And I feel it deep within my soul.

Christie
Too
I think

These are harsh times
My friends

This fear is JARRING
And it threatens to eat you for breakfast

BUT MY HOPE DOESN'T LIE IN MY SECURITY.

And neither should theirs.

But maybe they just need someone who'll listen.

Sometimes

Life is full of sometimes.

Sometimes, we find moths instead of butterflies.
Sometimes, we slog through swamps instead of skipping
    through puddles.
Sometimes, it's enough to just acknowledge you feel yucky.
Sometimes, people smash our hearts on the ground when we
    trust them.

But sometimes, they plant trees in our souls and help us
    cultivate them.
Sometimes, there is beauty in our ugliness.
Sometimes, while our feet are swishing their way through the
    unimaginable, we discover new life.
Sometimes, a soft and gentle beauty is better than the one we
    were hoping for.

There's no way to know which sometimes will happen,
But sometimes, all of life, and all its beauty, can be found in a
    single breath.

Green Eyes

Some might call you Green Eyes
When they see what you treat tender as a dove,
But there's something they don't realize.

They take a look at your brand new prize.
It might seem heaven-sent from above;
Some might call you Green Eyes.

"Do you see all the things he buys?"
They ask; their judgment, you are undeserving of,
There's something they don't realize.

Your material wealth runs to the skies,
But there's no mention of friends thereof.
Some might call you Green Eyes.

You are begging for someone to sympathize.
What good is money if you have not love?
There is something they don't realize.

You can't stop it, no matter the number of tries,
So you don your new diamond-laced gloves.
Some might call you Green Eyes,
But there's something they don't realize.

Calamity Ensues

You weren't expecting IT
You would never expect IT
But IT happened
And IT left you breathless

Your soul took a jolt of 2,000 volts
And somehow, you're still alive
But you maybe don't feel like you are

You walk through life at half a mile an hour
While all the other people zoom past you in Ferraris
Not a single drop of feeling passes through your thirsty lips –
    except when
Pain knocks on the doors of your heart in the middle of the
    night
And doesn't stop until morning
Not even when your eyes run out of tears

But He makes beauty from unfeeling ashes
Stepped and stomped on by unfeeling hearts
And He is near to the brokenhearted
He knits each piece back together with care
These are promises you can trust in the midst of the worst
    calamity imaginable
In the midst of that IT that happened to you

And you can trust that your worth is not defined by what you've
    done
Or what's been done to you
God sees you as pure and lovely
The way He created you to be

And one day
When IT has been wiped completely from the slate of your life
You will look back and see how far Love has brought you
You will look back and know what He saved you from
And that saving grace will lead you in all your ways
Not just today, but in all your days to come
From now until the end

Dragging Down[11]

Feet glued to the pavement
Lagging behind
Everyone flying past you

Wading through deep waters
Rushing past you ever faster
Sweeping you off your feet

Bricks tied around you[12]
Dragging you into The Deep
Can't breathe – losing air

Weights braising your body
Tied to your legs, your stomach, your arms
Can't get free

But something breaks through the night
Something breaks through your plight

And you're seeing the Sun
And you're feeling His peace
And He's telling you it's okay
And He promises another day

The light doesn't fade
It grows brighter and more steady
And as you watch it longer
Everything else falls away
The weights that once held you

---

11 This poem is partially inspired by "The Pheonix" by Fall Out Boy
12 This comes from a lyric from that song – "You are a brick tied to me
that's dragging me down."

Now hold you no longer
And you can see what's around you
And your lungs can breathe the air again

You're not quite sure what that light is
Or who might have sent it
All you know is you're grateful for it
And the freedom it brought to your soul

Anger is Darkness

Anger is darkness
The more you have
The less you remember
In the moment
Rage is all you feel
Then it's over
And *nothing*
It leaves you empty every time

Anger bleeds darkness
Dripping putrid dampness down your spine
Dripping fear and hatred in your mind
Dripping madness into your heart

Anger breeds darkness
Creating insanity in you
Recreating it in them
And recreating it again
Reaching further and further
And never ending

Anger frees darkness
With every minute you spend in rage
Your sight of what is true becomes more lost
And as the Truth recedes
So does its light
Until it is but a speck on the horizon

Anger is darkness
Make yourself stop
Close your eyes
Walk away from that moment

Take a breath and let it go
Step toward that horizon
And you'll find Truth's light will grow

Anger is only a feeling
Do not let it reign in your heart
Step toward the light once more
The light will grow
Then step again
And it will grow again

Leave anger in your dust as you rid yourself of it
Running, leaping, and shouting for joy
And the light you once ran from
You run for it now
Not looking back until
The light consumes you

Then you when look back
The anger will be gone
And its darkness will be imprisoned by the light

Daunting Darkness
First published on meglynch203.wordpress.com: 13 July, 2016

> "The rain clouds are thick tonight.
> All you can see are the car lights."

Last night's drive home was a dreary one. It wasn't late enough to be dark yet, but the clouds were so dense I could barely see around me. At first, it bore fear, tearing its way quickly to my stomach.

It was a different kind of darkness. There was no moonlight to spread warmth through the night, no stars twinkling the way. There was only a stark blackness, broken by flashing reds, greens, and yellows.

It was a quiet darkness, but not quite peaceful. Traffic was slow, winding silently through the streets, but the darkness was all-encompassing. Everything was black; there were no charcoal grays outlining the treetops or the open path of the road.

It was a crowded darkness. Man-made colors glowed steadily, then were gone – changing methodically, rhythmically, surely. Brake lights blazed through my retinas, blinking left and right, time to stop.

After a second thought, the darkness shifted. There was still a lack of natural light to break the monotony, but a single realization broke its hypnosis. This darker darkness holds nothing the normal darkness doesn't. More blackness does not equal more badness. I will make it home safe and sound.

It was never a darkness issue. It was a heart issue.

As I pushed away the dreariness, the fear abated. The blazing lights dulled and showed me the way home. I met the darkness with the understanding that all storms pass, and I knew that I would meet the sun upon waking this morning.

These are the Scars[13]

There once was a time
When life didn't hand you lemons.
It chucked 50-pound cartons of them straight at your heart
So hard and fast you could never duck away

And that blast left you reeling
With open wounds, bleeding
And your soul took a beating, too.
You took yourself to a doctor,
And the doctor fixed you up,
But the doc who healed your body, well,
He couldn't heal your soul.

So you found yourself in a place wondering,
What's one more open wound?
You let the razor slip through the cracks.
You thought the burning feeling
Was a new sort of healing,
But it wasn't.
It only ever left you empty
And emptier.

But then you found the Light,
And the Light turned everything right.
He taught you how to love the ones around you
And yourself most important of all.
He showed you the value of a heart made whole,
And He stitched up your bleeding soul.

---

13   This poem is inspired by this lyric from the song "Always" by Switch-
foot – "These are the scars deep in your heart…"

And so you've found healing,
And God has blessed your heart.

But His people, you could do without.
They look at you and shiver,
Disgusted,
Because how could any ever…?

But what they don't see is
Every mark etched on your skin
Reflects a mark etched in your soul
They could never understand the pain you were forced to live
    with,
The burdens you were forced to bear with no respite.

But the Light,
That Good, Good Shepherd,
He looks at you and sees the pain He washed clean away.
He looks at you and believes,
"You are who you are, and even your scars are lovely."[14]

---

14 This quote comes from the song "Scars" by Chris Sligh.

Chains

Look for your chains,
Those nagging thoughts
That bewitch your mind.

You can't...No good...Despicable

Seek out your chains,
Those haunting, nagging ghosts
That tear you down.

I know what you did last night...last week...last year.

Hunt for your chains.
Knock them out of hiding
Bring them into the light.

You will never–

Spend time seeking in all directions.
Look inward and see
They reside only in your mind.

silence

Search earnestly for your chains.
"Look for your chains.
They're not really there."[15]

---

15   My good friend Gina Viarruel said this in an interview.

Let Love Lead

Anger took hold of my heart again
In an instant

It began with one little thing going wrong
My heart gave way to rage
And then everything there was
Made the anger grow

In only a second
Anger took root in my soul
And outgrew the sunshine with barbed shade
Dark clouds flew in
And the rays of light around me faded

But then there was another instant
I decided that anger would not be who I am
Love is the wave I ride

I pushed aside the radio
Instead of up-beats that would foster fury
I listened to Coldplay's calming rhythms

And moment by moment
The barbs sank away
Sunlight broke through
The storm clouds dispersed

And moment by moment
Peace swept further and further into my soul
Until all I knew was love

Back on my feet

The morning came and went again,
And so did my need for love.
My days lack friends,
And my nights are full of nightmares I can't get rid of.

I've spent days and months
And maybe even years
Stuck in this twister of highs and lows,
I'm sick of these stunts
Living in constant high gear
And bearing the weight of constant blows.

I know it won't be like this forever;
I ponder in hope at the days to come.
You never know what may come tomorrow,
But no good or bad can last forever.
You lose some, but you also win some.
I may have been swept off the road for now,
Stuck in nothingness and despair,
But the day will come when I find solid ground.
The day will come when I'm not gasping for air,
And my limbs will not be bound.

This is something I can beat
I will stand atop it, full of pride
Staring down at depression's filth.
"When I get back on my feet,
I'll blow this open wide
And carry me home in good health."[16]

---

16 This quote comes from the song "Who do you Love" by Marianas Trench.

The Drought

Atlanta, GA went through a three-year-long drought.
Us kids thought we were going to die,
But we all joked about doing The Rain Dance,
And we laughed as our spit boiled on the tar of the parking lot.

PRESERVE THE WATER
SAVE THE FISH
LET YOUR LAWN WITHER

Street-corner environmentalists out-numbered the street-corner
    preachers.
We couldn't eat out or enter a store without hearing about The
    Drought,
The parts we were playing in perpetuating it
And the parts we could play in stopping it.

I remember the day it broke.
The heavens opened,
And the water we'd needed for so long finally came tumbling
    down.
The blue summer sky turned dark in a single moment,
And we were baffled.

But the next moment, we felt wonderful.
It was like seeing snow for the first time.
What is this sweet magic falling from the heavens?

With every drop, a cooling sensation reminded us that Heaven
    cared.
Our thirsts were quenched.
Steam lifted from the asphalt as fat drops of perfection drizzled
    down our arms and into our ears.

The dust of too many daily grinds was erased from our glasses,
Swept away by the cleansing flood we'd prayed so hard for.

When we were kids, we didn't realize The Drought could be a
    thing of the heart.
Droughts of the heart hurt worse, I think.
With a water drought, you know how to fix it.
Atlanta took some water from a river and sent it to Florida to
    help them out; they had it worse.
With a love drought, you can't always tell.
You can't steal love from someone else and make your own
    heart feel any better.

Our losses leave us breathless,
And we can get lost in the breathlessness,
Lost in our loss,
Lost in our never-even-receiving-to-begin-with.

We can never reverse death,
But there can be New Life.
There WILL be New Life.
There will come a moment when your lungs open, and you can
    breathe again.
The aches and pain will be washed away with the tide of new
    mercy for the days that lie ahead.

There will come a day when the loss does not define you.
Like Job in the wilderness, we will regain what we've lost a
    hundred fold.
Peace will reign in the land of our hearts,
Gushing forth with the sustaining beauty of joy,
Fed by The Everlasting Thunderstorm of Love.

I promise it's there.
I promise it's coming.
Trust in Love; He is faithful to send the rain.

Green: Hear the Sound

"Life is now;
This is our moment.
Hear the sound of hope that is calling.
No more waiting;
The door is open…
This is our moment."

MIKESCHAIR, "This Is Our Moment"

45¢

Forty-five cents sowed into a pond

FAITH

And an anthem building to one very specific crescendo in a human's life

HOPE

And He Who Promised is faithful.

LOVE

The Joy of a Little Girl

I experienced a little girl yesterday morning, playing with a frisbee in front of a café. Her mom brought out her smoothie when it was ready.

Her eyes would have lit up in joy…if they weren't already.

That's how I want to live my life, so full of joy that when joyful things happen, I can't express it any stronger than I am now.

Don't Let Them Win

A portrayal of what it feels like to have anxiety

You can't let them win
The people who've hurt you
And then hurt you even worse
But there's nothing you can do to stop them

Don't let them bury you
Lying desperate in an empty grave
Flecks at first sprinkling
Then raining
Then torrenting down upon you
Can't climb out
The weight is too heavy
Can't even breathe

Don't let them burn you
Fire, fire burning bright
Yellow and orange all around you
Darkness above
Inhaling smoke
Not exhaling the fear

Don't let them scar you
Hanging, open-armed, upon a wooden cross, alone
No one to save you
No one even cares
Rakes torn down upon your open flesh
Too much to be seen
Nowhere to hide

Don't let them see your heart
You know nothing good can be found there

So why even give them the chance?
You are the epitome of worthless
As every person has convinced you to believe

Don't let them know your pain
They will make it worse
Their judgment will rain down from the heavens
Saying how much you are not worth
Saying how you should be gone by now

Don't let them win
Don't let them in

~

Author's note: This poem is meant to show what it feels like to live your life guided by anxiety. It can often be a very tangible thing, especially for someone with a vivid imagination who was never taught healthy dreaming. This is not a healthy life model; please do not take this to condone your anxiety. Take every thought captive to Christ.[17]

Please let me ensure you that each of these images is a stark lie. Hear the hope that is calling you here. It doesn't matter how deep your cuts run; if you have believed in Christ's sacrifice for your soul, you have been set free by grace. That is a Capital-P Promise. You are loved beyond measure, unconditionally, forever. That's another Promise.

One thing I've learned: The only thing that can heal the worldview that says all people are horrible maniacs who are out to get you is to meet and know people who aren't. Vulnerability can be a terrifying thing; you can believe me when I tell you I

---

17   This can be found in the verse 2 Corinthians 10:5.

know that. Anxiety is a terrible monster to battle, but you don't have to battle it alone.

If you have no one else, you have me. My contact information and some hotlines are in the back of this book. Please seek help.

And know that you are loved.

Terror and Truth

Faith is terrifying.
Am I allowed to say that?

Leaping, jumping, trusting
With no solid ground to land on—
It's scary

The fear might drown you
The vulnerability might drain you
The darkness might overcome you

It's ugly
But it's beautiful

Soaring outwards
Or trembley-stepping, toe-by-toe
To an end you'd never imagine
But knew would happen all along
Your hope now is not for nothing

If you didn't have fear
You wouldn't need faith
True faith lies in the unknowing
In the terror-filled moments

Like that moment on the invisible bridge[18]
You've just gotta believe

We believe the truth that sets us free
The truth that beckons us forward into all goodness

---

18   This refers to a moment in the movie *Indiana Jones and the Last Crusade.*

The truth that deserves all or nothing
The truth that He will never leave us or forsake us[19]

It whispers in the stillness of the morning
Come to me and be filled
Be strengthened
Renewed
Prepared for the day

You cannot see Truth
But it sounds melodious
It is sweet-smelling
Its breath is gentle

Truth brings peace
And that peace negates the terror
Wherever it goes
Calmness trails in its wake
Twinkling like dewdrops in the atmosphere

Where can terror hide
When Truth is near?
It cannot face the glory unscathed

No matter the circumstance
No matter how great the fear monster is
Truth wins

---

19 This concept comes from the verse Deuteronomy 31:6.

I know your type.

I know your type.

Head down
Toughen up
Pressing on
Sideways glances at the people you know are watching you fail

But it's not just that –
They're watching you fail at failing, and they're judging you as
    less-than
You hear their whispers from afar
They hate you

I know your type.

As they watch you climb out of your failure, they laugh
They watch you slip and fall, and they do nothing to help
Because they know you'll never make it
You will never get out of the pit you've buried yourself in
Surely your fall was your fault

I know your type.

You never saw that miserable fall coming
But now it doesn't matter whose fault it was
Because you can't see a way out, no matter how desperately you
    try

The struggle that you wade through
The burden you carry on your back –
The one you're too scared to let go of –
It defines every inch of your mind

But the grace passed down from the Father
Through the Son
By the power of the Spirit
Refines every corner of your soul

I know your type.

You are so desperate for *something* to save you
You never imagined there was someONE who could
But there is!

I was your type.

I have been bogged down
Clogged up
Treated like a dog

I have been broken, bruised, and shattered
Beyond all recognition

But that grace I spoke about?
It's a driving force that builds you up and never tears you down

Supernatural grace broke into my world
It smashed its way through the window
Fixing all the pieces together in the process

I *was* your type.

My life was changed
When I let Love in
I let go of my baggage
To grab hold of something bigger
Something better

Love gave me a place to belong and proved His feelings for me
    are true
He helped me drop my baggage
Consume it in flames
And throw the ashes off a cliff
And Love has not left my side, not even once

I know your type.

The moment you meet Love
Will be the moment your life turns right-side-up

With tears in your eyes
You will step into the light
And people will see you as you are –
Too loved to be fathomed
Too beautiful to be tamed

And your type will change to
Who You Were Created To Be

In that singular moment
Those people who judged you wrongly
Well, their judgment just won't matter compared to Love's
    definition of You

I was your type.

I promise this is not over yet
There is always new hope
A dawn to come on the horizon and light your way through the
    darkness

Over time, that pit you've fallen into
Will dissipate into a blip too small to even stumble over

Trust in Love; He will not fail
Let Him renew your broken soul
His captivating perfection will wash away all your scary mess
And you will be pure as freshly fallen snow

Then that will be your type, just like it is my type now.
Clean. Cherished. Favored.
You can count on that.

Midnight Musings
First published on meglynch203.wordpress.com: 1 April, 2016

I just really need Jesus today.

I mean, I need Him every day. It's just…today, I feel like I need Him more.

It's been almost a month since I've posted, or since I've even written anything. I've just been so stressed out about money (what else is there to stress about?) and bogged down by my body's reaction to pollen (which, you really don't even want to know).

And tonight, about half an hour before I was going to turn in a job application, I went to the site to find it closed. I mean, I NEED this job, right? But I failed. I couldn't even fill out and turn in ONE STINKIN' JOB APPLICATION. I found out about it like a month ago. It's not like I haven't had the time to do it.

So I found myself in this cycle of anger and disappointment and fear and anger and disappointment and fear and anger and…oh, you get it.

But then it kind of stopped a little?

I had to stop for gas tonight because I have an important meeting in the morning and didn't want to worry about stopping. I had to spend money that I don't think I have…just another reason I won't make it to the end of the month, right? As I was pulling out of QT, there was this homeless guy standing on the corner, right next to a McDonald's. I felt God leading me to offer to get him something. I hesitated, but I had to stop.

You know what?

I offered this guy his choice of the entire menu, and all he asked for was a single ONE SINGLE sausage and egg biscuit. I yelled at him across the driveway, "WHATEVER YOU WANT, I'LL GET IT."

~hmm~

Uhh, just one sausage and egg biscuit, please.

I've found myself recently ordering more than my fill because I know other people are going to pay. Instead of a couple scrambled eggs, I'll get them with cheese, a waffle, and hot chocolate. Waffle House might be cheap, but at midnight, it's still more than I need, more money than they need to spend just because I want the taste of it in my mouth.

I've always prided myself in being able to receive what's given to me (because if someone wants to bless you, you should let them, right?), but I don't think I've been truly grateful for it, not recently, at least.

A haphazard THANKS! seems enough in the moment, but if I don't live it out, is it gratitude?

Just one sausage and egg biscuit will be fine.

It seems to me that I've been given all the oceans of the world, and I've settled to play in a puddle. While I am very grateful for the puddle, the oceans are right there waiting.

Something's been building in my heart recently, and I think I'm standing on the edge of a cliff, wearing one of those outfits that makes people look like a flying squirrel.

I'm about to start using my craft...finally. Don't get me wrong. Writing of any sort is using that craft. I just think it's about to be the time I use that craft as my source of income. I have no idea what this is going to look like just yet, but it's going to happen, and hopefully soon.

I'm content where I am, but I'm also longing for something more...still just a little too scared to look up from the puddle to find the oceans. Will they really be there when I lift my gaze?

Just one sausage and egg biscuit?
I bought him two.

Because to whom much is given, much is required...but that really wasn't much, was it? Six bucks...that is 1/7 of my phone bill, 1/35 of my car payment, and roughly 1/60 of what I spend on my own food a month.

It's also a lot less than what my friends have bought for me, and so much less than my parents have given me. I live at home, rent free. It's a miracle I've made it this far this way. I don't know where I would be if I didn't have my mom or my Gina or my Blair or my Julia or my...yeah, you get it.

Just one sausage and egg biscuit.
How could I not?

My Gina recently shared a nugget of wisdom with me – more than once, actually. I tend to forget and have to hear it over and over...

Gina buys all our food. We go play pool once a week, and we're at Waffle House every Friday after Ekklesia. She doesn't make a big deal out of it or anything, but if the waiter/waitress asks if we need the check split, she always says no. If the check is brought as one, she'll just slip her credit card down or slink off with the receipt to pay…and don't even think of touching your wallet if it's your birthday.

I asked her how she does it. I mean, we work in the same place; we make the same wage…and she can do all that for all those people? I know it's not just me or even just our group – It's everyone Gina comes into contact with.

Do you know what she said?

I just keep giving, and God just keeps providing. It's crazy.

She says this with the biggest smile on her face, like she can't wait to tell the next person about how giving has changed her life. She doesn't have to worry about money at all because it's just a cycle of giving, giving more, and giving even more.

How lovely is that?

Just a sausage and egg biscuit,
and I'll throw in some fries you didn't even know you wanted.

Because the beauty of giving is that there is always enough.
I saw a man praying with the homeless guy as I passed them on my way out. $20 says it's the same guy I gave some food to later last year just across the road from this same McDonald's. Same height, same build, same smile with the missing "teefs."

And it gave me hope.

The world might not spin on the axis of six bucks, but six bucks is enough to change a life completely.

Tender Tingles

The rain feels like magic
Tender tingles on my skin
Now resting on my forearms
My open-waiting palms

The rain feels like magic
Tap-tap-tapping against my headphones
Rapping in time to a heavenly song
Sapping life-born ache from my joints

The rain feels like magic
As the storm takes a turn
I know the worst is yet to come
And wait for it with glee

The rain feels like magic
Tender tingles here
Plopping on my upturned face
Running in rivulets down my arms and legs

The rain feels like magic
I know no one can hear me
So I scream-sing along with every song
I know every word and hit every note with perfection

The rain feels like magic
As I adopt a graceless dance
Splashing in every single puddle
Not skipping a single beat as lights flicker across the street

The rain feels like magic
I can feel the heat of lightning

As it plays across the sky
I maybe should be scared, but I am fearless

The rain feels like magic
And I linger in this freedom
These tender tingles grant me joy
The smile on my face will not soon leave

The rain feels like magic
Even as I slow myself to a crawl and rebecome an adult
I must press against the notion
This was a waste of time

The rain feels like magic
These tender tingles remain
Even after I've stepped into the house
And replaced my soaked clothes with a warm, fluffy blanket

The rain feels like magic
As the minutes after dancing turn into hours
The sound of the clouds' pounding reserves lulls me into deep,
    renewing sleep
I can rest assured, knowing the morning will bring new mercy
    once again

Toughing it Out

Decisions, decisions,
A thousand decisions,
And some that you make are just dumb.

But other decisions,
Well, they mean the world.
They have power to make it or break it.

Our decisions are dominoes,
One, two, three…
They affect the patterns of humanity.

We don't even notice
That with each choice,
Our whole worlds are shaped.

We don't see any effects in the moment,
But patience is a virtue,
After all.

Think about five years in the past.
Are you where you were then?
Are you the same human you used to be?

The time is now;
Take this moment life has given you.
Be the change you wish to see.

And after five years of decisions,
You'll look back and know:
You can be the person you hope to be.

In the Darkness, Be the Light

In the darkness, be the light
Shining fiercely into the night
And breaking through cloud barriers
Nothing can stop your fight

In the rage, be the peace
Help the kindness around you increase
Be gentle to the souls around you
And your joy will never cease

In the blandness, be the spice
Don't you dare think twice
About being the life of the party
Walk with an air of paradise

In the quiet, be the storm
Stir up that pot – let the chaos form
And then watch as life starts to thrive
And let all your fierceness roar

In the darkness, be the light
Stand up for others in their plight
Lay down your false security
And fight for what you know is right

Somewhere Over Thataway[20]

A whispered word – This poem is for you.

Somewhere over thataway,
All our deepest dreams lie hidden so close we can taste them,
Though we're not close enough just yet.

And somewhere over thataway,
Light-hearted banter ensues around a fireplace.
We will find the ones we love singing songs of hope.

Somewhere over thataway,
We will find security in letting go of all we know.
For we know so little, after all.

Somewhere over thataway,
The scales will fall away from our eyes,[21]
Leading to discovery of all the lovely things this earth has to
    offer that we never knew existed.

Somewhere over thataway,
We find hope of a future for the world much grander than the
    one we know.
No matter what happens, we know it will go on.

Oh, what a wonderful world we live in!
With stars in the sky every night and a sun that rises every
    morning,

---

20   This poem is inspired by the song "Somewhere Over The Rainbow/
What A Wonderful World" by Israel Kamakawiwo'ole.
21   In Acts 9, Saul, persecuter of Christians, had an encounter with
Christ, and his blinded eyes were then made whole as the "scales" fell
away from them.

How can we not hold on to better days?

The colors and sounds of life around us bring joy,
Such joy we can hardly bear it.
And we will know love each day with every breath we take.

Somewhere far above us, up and over thataway,
We know that Love calls us by name
For Love Himself has brought us here to dream these dreams
and live this life.

And somewhere of thisaway,
These truths grant us peace and resiliency to fight the long
battles ahead.
We know Love's Promises will not leave us alone.

Why
Oh why
Can't you dream this, too?

Better Together

In ministry and life
In conflict and strife
We belong together

When our worlds are breaking
And it seem the earth is shaking
We need each other

For when darkness is near
And all you feel is fear
You won't make it through with just you

The only thing that will save you
When you have no idea what to do
Is togetherness

If we have not each other, what else is there?
Only burdens we could never bear
Our friends and their love is all we need

Find a community you love
That will help you rise above
Standing steadfast together

For when we live alone
That's when Satan brings trouble unknown
And our loneliness overwhelm us

But when we live with friends
We find joy that never ends
And our faith in Love grows deep

Being with each other makes us stronger
And we find fear no longer
We are better together, forever

Becoming More[22]

WIDE-EYED

We enter this world curious.
With wide eyes filled with wonder, we think,
What on earth can this big, beautiful place not offer me?

With reckless abandon, we run
Regardless of all pain to come.
What in this big, beautiful place can hurt me?

As children, we are here to testify:
The glory of the One cannot be mistaken.
Who else could create such a big, beautiful place?

MYSTIFIED

We grow weary of this life
After too many falls and broken hearts
What on this earth is good?

Yet the One who walks with us knows our hurt
And loves us even if it is our own fault.
Is there nothing I can do that will shake You away?

We find it is the ups and downs that make life amazing
Somehow, some way, each moment is beautiful
Wherever shall I go next?

---

22   The structure of this poem is based loosely on the song "The More"
by the band Downhere and its coinciding albums: *Wide-Eyed and Mystified*
and *Wide-Eyed and Simplified.*

SIMPLIFIED

Our frightful plight falters
As we realize Who is for us
You will overcome everything for my good.

Our weariness turns to confidence
We take life as it is and start giving back
You created me to do this.

And all of life falls into place
As we step out in faith and fortitude.
You will never leave my side; we are eternally united.

Even Though

*First published on meglynch203.wordpress.com: 9 November, 2015
inside the post "The Thirty Day Poem Challenge: Day 11"*

Even though there has been a lot more pain than anyone would ever think there would be, there is so much beauty here, too. Even though we sometimes miss the sunset because we still have too much to do that day, it doesn't mean it isn't there. Even though we don't see the butterfly we can be while the world is closing in on our caterpillar selves, it doesn't mean that isn't what we're turning into. And even though the pain can be too much to bear at times, so can the beauty.

There is always beauty in every storm, and no matter how much we see it or not – it exists. Everything that matters hurts; everything that matters is beautiful.

Blue: The Winner's Circle

"Love woke me up this morning,
And I ran to see the king in the winner's circle
On the horse he won for me."

Bethany Dillon, "Dreamer"

The Good Word

Darkness is the beginning of all things.
The world itself was formed from bleak nothing.
But a Word was spoken,[23]
"Let there be light,"[24]
And thus the world was born.

And with one Word,
An all-of-life-long promise was made.
The very stars numbered the descendants of just one I'm-too-
broken couple
The sea was split in two to make a way.
A dancing king with a heart of gold taught us about
redemption.
A weeping prophet foretold destruction but assured His People
they would be renewed.
A harlot was saved from her life of woe, proving His Goodness.
And His Perfect Restoration brought forgiveness a thousand
times before it was finished.

And with one Word,
All creation shifted.
As a grace-filled King was laid in a manger with no room left
for Him elsewhere,
Angels paraded the Good News across the sky.
And many came to worship the tiny, worth-filled child.

And with one Word,
A sacrifice was made.
The veil that separated us was torn.

---

23 John, the disciple of Jesus, refers to him as the Word in John 1.
24 This quote comes from the verse Genesis 1:3.

Mercy – a definition

First published on meglynch203.wordpress.com: 1 November, 2015 with the title "The Thirty Day Poem Challenge: Day 4"

n.

an idea(l)
1. forGIVEness
2. a love undeserved
3. a debt forsaken
4. a death foretaken

v.

mercying
1. showing
2. trusting
3. understanding
4. loving, despite

adj.

mercy-full
1. a state of being
2. constancy in giving, loving, caring
3. remission of pride|influx of humility

A Father's Hug

I'm in need of a father's hug
A snatch-you-from-your-fears embrace
That wipes all terror away
And teaches me I'm loved

I need a hug from mi Padre
A soul-ravishing squish of affection
That makes every inch of you feel loved beyond measure
With a love that breaks down every single barrier

I need a proper hug from Daddy
A pick-you-up-and-swing-you-around celebration of our love
That goes beyond all we could ever ask or imagine
And erases every doubt of its Truth

Before the Rain

Empty
Weightless
    But waste-full

Dirty knees
Smudged glasses
Gross-feeling heart

Hidden in darkness
Afraid of the light
Ashamed of too much

Doomed to stay here
Cannot stay here
Must stay here

Anxiety – I HAVE TO FIX THIS NOW
Depression – I just cannot fix this
Fear – What if it never gets fixed?
Despair – It can never be fixed
Together, at once

There is no way out
There is just this
Nothingness

In the Thunderstorm

Stand under the tall trees and listen to the slower dripping of
the rain.
Splash in all the puddles and feel yourself half-drowning in the
wetness of the air.
Feel the air clear as the raindrops wash away the smog.
Watch the depth in the clouds zooming over your head.
Know how small you are.

It's invigorating, and it's beautiful.

After the Rain

Calm, cool serenity now

Free breathing
Vibrant colors
Dampened senses
Fresh air
Clear mind
Grassy toes
Petrichor

Muddy puddles
Ankle-deep
Draining to the sewer
Bringing all the angry angst with it

Excess drip – drip – dripping
Washing away the dirt of too many days
Pulling tension from the atmosphere of the earth
And the atmosphere of your heart

Holding hands with freedom
As life comes flooding back
But the burdens stay where you've left them
Never to be carried again

A Prayer for Her

Father, protect her all her days.
Let her wanderings be guided by Your ever-steady hand;
Lead her far away from temptation,
That she not fail at the break of day: morning, afternoon,
    evening, night.

Father, build her house and keep all her family safe.
Hold them close inside the palm of Your hand;
Enclose them in Your Promises, Your plans for their lives.
Shelter them forever in Your wing.

Father, grant her mercy.
This, she does not deserve, but neither do I.
You have done so much for me; I ask only that You share the
    same for her.
Are we not both Your children?

Father, bring her home.
You are the Good Shepherd who leaves the ninety-nine to go
    and find the one.
You know where she sleeps, where she steps, where she dances;
Please guide Your prodigal back to her safe haven.

Father, keep that lovely, home-coming day close to my heart,
That I not forget her beautiful soul.
Let me not forget how she helped me;
Let me help her when she calls.

Father, lead her to Your heart.
Teach her how loved she is no matter the mistakes she's done or
    thought or said.

Envelope her forever in Your unconditional, agape passion for
her,
And don't You ever leave her side.

Amen

Rainbows on My Heart

First published in The Taste of Words: This is only the beginning 2014, 2016

I see rainbows on my heart
Beautiful and lovely
Full of the glory of the Almighty
He lives in me
He is my reason for life
The breath in my lungs
The blood in my veins
The color of my skin
The light in my eyes
The very best in me

Red to violet
He's in every aspect of me
And who I'm becoming
The very best me I could ever be
A lover of people
A survivor
A fighter

I see rainbows on my heart
Countless colors
Countless people I have loved
Each person is a part of who I am
A part of this "me"
I am a culmination of who I've known
Who I have loved
And who I have not loved
They all have touched this heart in different ways

I see rainbows on my heart
A sun-lit storm
This life roars on
A light this world will never put out
Dimmed, perhaps
But always there to guide a lonely sailor home

I see rainbows on my heart
And I am humbled by love
This all-consuming love sent by my Father
I know who I am
Where I am going
Because of this love
His sacrifice
Of greatest price

These rainbows on my heart
All the beauty of who I am
Comes from this love
I am who I am only because He loved me

No More Paper Hearts

You know how some kids tear apart important papers and then
try to tape them back together?
Once torn, paper can never be what it was before,
Especially that sort-of-two-ply paper that not only rips by the
length or width but also the depth.
You can't fix that.
That's a fact.

But with all these dumb breakup songs, we've been treating our
hearts the same way.
We act like our souls are as fragile and fragmented as decade-old
wallpaper being shredded and tossed away.
We drop our heart pieces – our very beings – on the ground
and walk away because we find so little value in them.
Because someone else decided we weren't worth the time or
effort.
People will break you.
That's a fact.

But there is a God who loves you enough to give everything up
to strengthen you.
There's this Japanese art form called Kintsukuroi – They inlay
the broken parts of shattered pottery with gold. It makes
them stronger and so much more beautiful.
The more you are broken and heal, the more you become
golden.
It doesn't matter how badly you are broken. You can be made
new again.
He will heal you.
That's a fact.

If Hope has a Name

Hope shines bright in the night, the stars that guide sailors
home
It shines bright in the storm, the lighthouse that stops vessels
from death upon the rocky shore
It shines bright in the fear, the voice that assures, "You might be
down, but you're not out."
If hope has a name, it is light

Hope is pure and untamed, fighting tyrannical takeover with its
beautiful truth
Gently violent, it finds its way into every corner of your war-
torn heart to replace fear with peace
Love calms the flame of your pain with its fiery passion, no
more ache; only harmonious tranquility
If hope has a name, it is love

Hope combats evil with good
God became man to put a stop to hatred
He preached love with a heart moved by compassion
Even death itself stops bluntly before Him
If hope has a name, it is Jesus

David and Goliath

The human eye can see the light of a single candle from the length of a football field.

This revelation makes it easier to focus on the light instead of the dark, no matter how daunting or Goliath-like it seems.

I think that's it, though. That's where it's easy to let the darkness win. You're standing there, David-sized, and this overwhelmingly Goliath-sized thing envelops the space around you.

It can be so terrifying.

But in the moment David stood before his very real Goliath (a seven-foot, burley monster of a man), he knew nothing of fear. He knew only the power of God that resided within him. He was indignant at the insults Goliath threw his way, refusing to allow him to speak about God or His people the way he did.

The only thing that can get us shining again is the thing we already have. David, who became the King of Israel, pulled out his slingshot and, in one go, killed the gargantuan man who had disgraced Israel and vowed to destroy him.

The Bible says Goliath fell on his face, the stone sunk into his head, and his people ran for cover.[25] As they ran, the Israelites pursued. David's moment of victory spread to his people, and even they ran out in boldness.

---

25 You can find this story in 1 Samuel 17:48-51.

There's a thing David knew that maybe you don't yet. Nothing on this earth can defeat God. There is no losing when He directs the stones from your sling.

Your circumstances might seem to be Goliath compared to you, but with God on your side, nothing can stop you, and your victory is not yours alone. When people see how we've stepped up and overcome, they will be encouraged in their struggle, and with God on their side, they will win, too.

God is consistently fighting battles on our behalf we don't even know about, and He holds the keys of Death and Hell.

He waits for us in the Winner's Circle.

The Greatest Treasure

The greatest treasure is a sweet spring afternoon
Honeysuckle budding just around the corner
The sun shining brightly, eagerly, urging the world to begin
   anew

The greatest treasure is a bird perched in a tree
Singing the songs its soul longs to share
Enriching the air around it with joy

The greatest treasure is a bed of lush, green grass overflowing
   with wildflowers
A celebration of life playing quietly along the footpath
Beckoning travelers to a most undignified dance party

The greatest treasure is light permeating the darkness within
Natural light found in a windowless office
Acceptance of the sweetest invitation

"The greatest treasure is an empty tomb"[26]
Hope found when all seems lost
New life after the old was stolen

---

26 This lyric comes from the song "Excavate" by Downhere.

Indigo: We Will Sing

"I will sing of all You've done.
I'll remember how far You've carried me.
From beginning, to the end,
You are faithful, faithful to the end."

Bethel Music, "Faithful to the End"

Spirit, Come

Come, Precious Holy Spirit
Join us here and now as we praise Your holy name
Find pleasure in our song and dance
Receive the blessings pouring out from us to You
We do not have much, but what we do have is Yours

Alight here with us in this time
Delight in our praise of all You've done
Hear our songs of love for You, the One Who First Loved
Let our worship never fade away
Let us never forget the beauty of Your Truth

Come and perch atop our mustard trees
Our faith is rich, with deep roots, strong trunks, and healthy
    branches
Help us cultivate a garden full of good fruits and gorgeous
    flowers
Help us become a pleasing aroma
So that all who come might find you

    Dwell deep within each moment until all we know is You
Abide in our hearts until all we feel is Your peace and
    protection breathing in,
Your patience and grace breathing out
Reside in our souls until all our hope resides in Your Promises
    come to pass
Spirit, come – until all we are aligns with the beauty of Your
    Love

A Fire Kind of Beautiful

It lounges on a couch
Eyes closed, senses ready
Feeling and hearing instead of seeing her surroundings
Listening intently to what is actually going on – deeper than
    surface level

It perches on a stool
Ready to jump up and help at a moment's notice
She cherishes the lives around her, and so
She waits for their cries of pain – not just physical

It wanders free
Straying to the stairway and beyond, to the kitchen area and
    back
Swaying to the music that surround sounds her with His praises
But she stays close to her friends – her framily

It settles on a table
Content to shift the purpose of furniture to fit the needs of her
    worship
Arms raised high in open surrender to the Only One
The Creator of Heaven and earth – of all that lives and
    breathes

Even So

The light around is darkening
Storm clouds cover the sky
Even so, I am safe

Cacti cover the ground
Stealing water from all around
Even so, I have life

Friends leave; lovers shy away
Loneliness has become my middle name
Even so, I am valued.

The Enemy comes
To steal, kill, and destroy
Even so, I am stable

Hatred rises all around me
Threatening to end my life
Even so, I am loved

The Gideon Effect

First published on meglynch203.wordpress.com: 18 November, 2016

I've always felt a certain love for Gideon, one of the men God chose to lead Israel into victory over the Midianites. The part where Gideon challenges God in his unbelief has stuck like Gorilla glue to the walls of my heart.[27]

After an angel foretold Gideon's leadership in victory over the Midianites, Gideon asked God to prove himself; he left a piece of wool outside overnight and asked that God leave the ground dry and only the wool wet with dew. In the morning, Gideon found the ground dry, and only the wool was wet. In fact, he squeezed an entire bowl full of water out of it! The next day, Gideon switched his request around, and God pulled through again – the ground was wet with dew, and the wool was bone dry. God changed the way nature works just to prove himself to Gideon.

When I was a kid, it was hard to believe it took that much convincing for Gideon to believe he could do it. If an angel of the Lord came and told me what to do, I would trust everything he said. No exceptions.

But in the spring of 2014, God began leading me in ways I never would have dreamed before, and when He did, I did not believe him. I had no confidence in my worth as a writer, as a friend, or even as a child of God. I became much like Gideon – seeing myself as the smallest person of the weakest clan.

That year was hard for me, my family, my friendships, and even my church life. A lot of tension built up in many ways, with no foreseeable reason as to why it all happened. September 2014

27   The story of Gideon's calling can be found in Jduges 6:11-27

remains the lowest point of my life thus far. With a father sick in bed, a job that did not pay me enough to live on, and waves of feeling deserted by people I'd known my whole life, there wasn't much that could make my life worse.

Then pastors everywhere I went, every podcast I listened to, and quotes sent from friends were talking about Gideon, and I was reminded of his challenge to the Lord. I remembered the fact that God changed the way nature works in order to prove himself to Gideon.

Sitting in a pew in my timidity, a few words felt their way out of my mouth, "Can I ask for that?"

One night a few weeks later, I asked again, and in the morning, I got my answer, but, of course, the significance was lost in the busyness of a late morning.

As I grabbed my shoulder bag to run out the front door, I heard a horrible, soggy squish. I yanked it open to find my journal warped with wetness. Its pages had more waves than the ocean! I snatched my Most Important Book, and the pages themselves cried their way through the house as I searched for a towel. I dropped the MIB in my bathroom sink because, well, there was nothing I could do, and there were other books to save.
But the only other wet thing I could find in my bag was the space at the bottom of the bag where my journal sat.

WHAT.

My hands combed their way around each item several times. Bone. Dry. The water bottle in the corner was still sealed closed, and the water was at full capacity. The pages of my tutoring handbook were not affected, and my tablet flashed on in an instant.

I did not have time for this. I grabbed my MIB, squeezed out as much water as I could, and left the journal to dry in the window of my car; it stayed there for months and was almost thrown away when I finally cleaned out my car. I had long moved on to another journal.

The next year, Gideon cropped his way back into my life, and I found myself asking again, "Can I ask for that?"

"Hmm?" God responded.

"Um, like Gideon did with the wool?"

"Huh," his amusement surprised me.

"You know, I asked for it a while ago. Nothing happened."

"You didn't see what I did there, did you?" an image of a huge, mischievous grin cropped into my mind.

God took me step-by-step through that morning before it hit me.

I asked for a Gideon moment, and the lovely Holy Spirit delivered.

As soon as I got home, I ran straight to the now-sacred journal. When I opened its pages, awe filled my soul. Of the thousands of written words, only three pages were affected. Three pages of overwhelming heartbreak and fear were washed away completely. There were quotes written in gel ink and doodles in

sharpie, both of which bleed…but not in my Gideon Moment.
God lit up my soul with the reality that, yes, he created me for
the extravagant dreams now residing in my heart. He erased
all doubt completely from my heart; I know for certain His
purpose for my life.

If God can move in a season when I felt like the smallest,
weakest person, when He knew I would be so busy I wouldn't
even notice, He can and will move for you, and He will do so in
phenomenal ways you can barely imagine He will.

I promise; you *can* ask God for that thing you've been hoping
for. One day, you'll wake up and see: that's how he did it, and it
will be the most beautiful thing you could ever dare to imagine.
You need not fear you'll miss it; He will reveal to You his works
in due, perfect time.

All you need to do is ask.

Faithful and True

In the background of my mind
Truth rings freely
Resounding throughout eternity
And residing in my heart

Faithful and true
You are faithful and true

In all the history of this earth
You are I Am
Your character never changes
Nor does Your Love for us

Faithful and true
You are faithful and true

Our hope is founded
On this Solid Rock
You died to win us our freedom
You died so that we might live

Faithful and true
You are faithful and true

Promises live where freedom reigns
And freedom reigns in Your love
And just as You fulfilled Your promises to Abraham, Isaac, and
    Jacob
So You will fulfill Your promises to me

Faithful and true
You are faithful and true
To me

May I Always
First published in The Taste of Words: This is only the beginning *2014,*
2016

May I follow Your loving hand
Surely in every step, every way,
Even through a thousand different lands.

Wrap Your love around me tightly, like a band
And set my heart ablaze.
May I follow Your loving hand.

Allow Your grace within me to expand,
And let me never leave Your gaze,
Even through a thousand different lands.

Give me hope in the morning so grand;
Together, the world we will amaze.
May I follow Your loving hand.

Give me nothing we cannot withstand.
Spread Your love through my life like the sun's rays,
Even through a thousand different lands.

May I always sing Your praise
May I love You always.
May I follow Your loving hands,
Even through a thousand different lands.

A Promise Everlasting

Everlasting is His justice

The heavens opened for the very first time
The rains came flooding down
 Tearing their way through humanity

Everlasting is His goodness

There was one He saw as faithful
And this man and his family, He saved
For He was unwilling to let the human race drop off completely

Everlasting is His provision

Forty days and nights passed in solemn darkness
As the world was covered in roiling waters
No hope was seen, but trust lingered there

Everlasting is His kindness

A dove was sent to find dry land
And in His goodness returned with an olive branch
The land bore fruit once more

Everlasting is His faithfulness

As Noah bent down to honor The Mist High, his prayer was
    rewarded
There will not be a curse upon all humanity ever again
Earth will revolve as it should without ceasing

Everlasting is His favor

"[God] literally made a new physical phenomenon
Just because He wanted to remind anyone who looked up after
    a storm
Of His loving kindness."[28]

And everlasting is His Promise

---

28 My friend Sarah Denton said this in an interview.

Daddy, Thank You

Daddy, I'm sorry.
I never seem to remember all the good things I am here to do
and all the good ways I can go about doing them.
Thank you for reminding me of my purpose and Your plan for
my life.

Daddy, I'm sorry that I hate other people when they hurt me,
or sometimes for no reason.
Thank you for forgiving the worst in me and helping me to
forgive in return.

Daddy, I never seem to find the time to share Your loving
message of hope with those who need it most.
Thank You for being the Healer of *all* our sick and weary souls.

I never seem to treat the world the way You meant for it to be
treated.
I never seem to see the people around me as the people You
know them to be.
I never seem to stop doing the things I know I should not be
doing.
I never seem to be the light on the hill You've asked us to be to
the valley.
I never seem to spread hope on the wings of eagles.
And I never seem to thank You for what You've done for me.

Daddy, thank You for loving me in all the little ways that mean
so much to me.
Thank You for seeing the potential in every moment and inside
of every soul.
Thank You for always being right here when I call.

For all I've seen and felt and known, thank You.
For all I never could have dreamed You did for me, thank You.
For everything under the sun, thank You.

Daddy, from the depths of my heart, I thank You.

We are like the Sky
First Published in The Taste of Words: This is only the beginning 2014, 2016

We are like the sky–
Our lives are but clouds
Stretching across eternity,
Maybe together
Maybe overlapped
Or maybe passersby

We are like the sky–
Our colors are but reflections of that which has passed through
    our lives
We are based on that which is the bluest of blues,
But our yellows and reds make oranges,
And once the mixing begins, it never ends.

We are like the sky–
We are constantly changing,
Churning our atmospheres into what was once unknown
And never will be known again.
Red and blue will always make purple,
But violet, plum, and lavender are far cries from each other.

We are like the sky–
What is true about me may be true about you, too.
All skies have stars, but not all in the same places.
Sometimes, all it takes to get to know someone
Is turning around to view from his perspective.

We are like the sky—
Happy or sad, or both at the same time.
Our happiness grows resiliently
In vibrant colors across our worlds.
Our sadness, in darkness, roars through space with
Maddening thunder and strokes of brilliant lightning.
But when those same times happen,
Rainbows do, too.
And that's how we know we've got it right.

We are like the sky—
Always beautiful, but sometimes fearsomely so.
Darkness breeds darkness and light, light.
Clouds may block the sun,
But new winds sweep through,
Bringing clarity once more.

To Make a Rainbow

What does it take to make a rainbow?
It is more than what it seems,
More than
C O L O R S
Lighting up the sky.

What does it take to make a rainbow?
Something tangible –
Water, glass, air
And something intangible –
Light
Bending and breathing through what we know
"It takes both to make this beautiful."[29]

What does it take to make a rainbow?
Artistry
Such creative prowess unmet by our human abilities
Rainbows hold all the colors we can see
In an arc that covers our entire sky as far as we can see
Who other than the One could have made such a thing?

What does it take to make a rainbow?
A promise set into the fabric of our atmosphere
Forever displayed across the sky:
"I have set my bow in the cloud,
And it shall be a sign of the covenant
Between me and the earth."[30]
A sign of His goodness until the end of the ages.

---

29 My friend Jordan Sanders said this in an interview.
30 This comes from the verse Genesis 9:13.

Lift your eyes

Lift your eyes from the depths
Lift your eyes up to the skies
As you wander along the open road
Away from all you've known before

Lift your eyes to new beginnings
Never turning back to the endings
For the whole world lies before you
A chaotic beauty that shares equal parts sadness and joy

Lift your eyes to the sweet summer sun
Beauty always comes after disaster
Even the darkest of nights has a dawn
Those April showers *will* bring the May flowers

Lift your eyes to the talents within your own soul
Everything you will need to get through life
Lies hidden deep within you
All you need to do is dig and find the treasure

Lift your eyes to good you will do
Armed with the power of the Holy Spirit
You will change the lives in this world for the better
Spreading love and erasing hate

Lift your eyes
Just lift your eyes

Violet: Here as in Heaven

"A miracle can happen now,
For the Spirit of the Lord is here.
The evidence is all around
That the Spirit of the Lord is here."

Elevation Worship, "Here as in Heaven"

Entrance to the Kingdom

There is a Kingdom Most Grande
With streets made of gold
And houses of ruby, emerald, and sapphire.
The air itself shimmers in grandeur
As a light no man can tame permeates the atmosphere.

Abundance resounds.
Food, warmth, and love are plentiful here.
No worries will you find.
You are cared for and well loved,
And this you will know deeply, fully.

Grace and mercy abound.
Echoes of laughter run through the air
Joined again and again forevermore.
Joy erases every frown;
Kindness dries every tear.

Fear abates at the loss of its threatening power.
Strength resonates throughout your body
As confidence grows anew.
As you walk through this Kingdom,
Peace is the freedom you find.

There are no taxes or tariffs.
You need only step in through the gate.
You smile and let go your baggage,
But nothing else need be done.
All you must do is come.

Let's Go Back, Dear

Let's go back to calling everybody "Dear."
Write everyone letters addressing them as close-to-our-hearts.
Let them hold our words in their hands
And be encouraged.

Let's go back to holding doors open for each other,
No matter how far they lag behind.
We'll bring people *with us*
As we walk into the world ahead.

Let's go back to not letting strangers be strangers for long.
Smiles and hugs make the world go 'round,
And we know everyone we meet
Needs at least one to last the day.

Let's go back to loving people regardless of limits,
Theirs or ours.
This is how they'll know us; this is how they'll see:
Our fully-functioning, unconditional love for each other.

From Here On Out

From here on out, we walk together.
Hand-in-hand, we will wander this earth,
Never leaving each other's side.
Our branches and roots will feed each other,
Sharing sunlight and soil as one.

From here on out, you will never be alone again.
All the pain you've known before,
You will not know any longer
Because your pain will be born on all our backs.
It will not weigh you down as before;
We will fly on wings as eagles
High above it all.

From here on out, your story will tell of amazing grace.
The ending you thought for sure was The Ending
Was a beginning all along.
How sweet the sound that saved you from destruction,
That made your broken heart brand new.

And we take

And so from here, we take all that we've learned,
As we waltz into the sunset
Better people than we were before.

And we take all the words I've shared,
Hold them close unto our hearts,
Every precious letter that has impacted our lives.

And we take all the tears we've shed,
Grateful for the healing that has taken place within our souls,
And we walk, smiling, into our destinies.

And we take all that we've heard,
And we let it change our hearts,
Making us stronger than even before we were broken.

And we take all that we've seen.
We find beauty in the ugliness,
For our ashes have been replaced with diamonds.

Gentle Whispers

First published on meglynch203.wordpress.com: 9 June, 2016 in the post titled "A Gentle Heart"

Gentleness whispers softly to us in that still, small voice:

Gentleness calls us to walk tenderly. *Be sweet.*

Gentleness floats toward us in the breeze, on silk-thin wings. *Bring them peace.*

Gentleness unloads freedom onto our hearts by the truckload and only asks that we spread it around. *Unlock their chains of defeat.*

Gentleness breaks the tension in our souls. *Tell them it's going to be okay.*

Gentleness promises to take away the pain. *Bind their brokenness with joy.*

Gentleness provokes us to walk this way. *Be the gentleness you wish to see in the world.*

And Help Me Have Mercy

First published on meglynch203.wordpress.com: 6 January, 2017

Lord, have mercy in my weakness.
You know my weary soul is desperate
For a touch of love no one can tear away,
And help me have mercy on all these lovely, weak humans

Lord, have mercy for the live-long morning
And all the frustration it holds.
When the house rumbles with resentment,
Grant us grace and make us whole,
And help me have mercy this morning.

Lord, have mercy for my rushing,
Heaving and ho-ing heart.
Bring Peace with You as we greet this day together.
Show me the patience it takes to spread love to weary hearts,
And help me kindle the sparks into proper fires.

Lord, pour Your mercy through this moment,
For each moment holds within in it
All the beautiful, worthy things we tend to overlook.
And these moments together, they mimic the sky-
Ever-shifting into a new sort of beauty.
Please help me not blink and miss it.

Lord, give me mercy when my life is not my own.
Help me learn the difference between
Living Your life and living others',
For freedom is found only on Your path least traveled.
And help me forge a trust in You that can never be taken away.

Lord, have mercy on this soul
That too quickly overlooks the things it should hold dear—
The people it should hold close.
Help me love them properly, as only You know how.

Lord, have mercy for today
And all the days to come,
And help me have mercy.

Almighty Presence

Like wading into the sun's rays on a hot summer day
After spending hours inside a frozen-with-air-conditioning
    house,
We step into Your presence.

Like waltzing through the house at midnight,
The only one awake,
We thrive in Your presence.

Like floating weightless in the Dead Sea
After a lifetime of too-heavy weights oppressing our shoulders,
We soak here in Your presence.

There is a sweetness here found nowhere else,
A cleansing rain that washes away all the mess of all the
    moments.
We rest here in Your presence.

You say we are free, chosen, loved.
You spread hope into our lives that cannot be erased.
We find out who we are here in Your presence.

We can't help but laugh in the face of danger
As Your JOY floods our souls.
We live in happiness in this place, Your Presence

Renewal overwhelms our souls.
We awaken with rigorous vigor to tackle the world ahead.
We walk in the strength of Your presence.

And in the midst of the tornadoes, volcanoes, tsunamis that
    flood our lives on a daily basis,
We close our eyes and step off into the world anew
Carrying Your almighty presence with us wherever we go

The Gathering Place

We have come to seek His face
We know we can find Him
Here at the gathering place

We have been mauled by sin's heavy mace
And our light is so dim
We have come to seek His face

With humble hearts, we approach this space
In His presence we'd like to swim
Here at the gathering place

But we feel He's vanished without a trace
Now, when our fate is most grim
We have come to seek His face

We wait here with a still pace
Singing everlasting hymns
Here at the gathering place

Lord, we need your grace
Our one and only Elohim
We have come to seek Your face
Here at the gathering place

No Other

No other love
Can reach our hearts the way Yours does

No other place
Can heal our souls like this place does

No other name
Can shake the nations as Yours

Let us love no other love
Let us stay in no other place
Let us sing no other name

The Pot of Gold

The pot of gold at the end of the rainbow is all any pirate longs
    for
The pot of precious commodity
The chest that holds all your dreams
The vessel withholding your life more abundant

People have spent all they have to just gaze upon it
They've spent entire lifetimes searching for it
They never gave up that search, even until their end
But that search has always proven fruitless

There's something they've all missed out on
The beauty they've searched dearly for all their lives resides
    nowhere other than the arms of Christ.
And the pot of gold at the end of the rainbow?
That's you.

There is beauty woven into every fiber of your being
It consists of the Most Holy of images
We were created by Love himself to be Love ourselves
In word and deed, in action and freedom

Did you know?
The pot of gold has been found – hidden in a field
The Son has trekked a long way to find you
And He died just to have the privilege of holding you

The Truth is that He lived a perfect life, never sinning even
    once.
Yet He was tortured for days

And He died a murderer's death upon a cross
And He rose from death three days later

He gave up everything He had
Just to have you near
And He would do it a thousand times over
And "Who pays a high price for nothing?"[31]

---

31 Christian teacher Dan Mohler says this a lot.

The Far Side of the Rainbow

Here you find yourself
At the end of your long journey,
Through all that needs to be said, for now.
Where do you go from here?

His sacrifice of greatest price
Has marked you forgiven.
It has marked you FREE.
Where do you go from here?

The oil of gladness
Smeared across your forehead,
The written word defining you now: BELOVED.
Where do you go from here?

Beauty has been found here,
Peace and glory, too,
Amidst all you've longed to be
Where do you go from here?

Nuggets of wisdom
Have passed through your fingertips
Like sand through an hourglass.
Where do you go from here?

Oh, Weary Wanderer,
Stand up on your feet.
Don your full armor.
Be still and know.
Hear his guiding whisper in your soul,
Where do we go from here?

One Liners

I think the greatest thing about being a writer is when I see something in a book—a single line—that must have meant the world to the author. I get those a lot, just one or two lines that sound to beautiful I could wrap myself in them like a blanket and go take a nap.

Steal the anger from my soul
And heal my soul from the anger

Blue is the color of a summer night
Right before the stars are overtaken by neon explosions.

The sun is scorching on my back
Beckoning me forward in all that I lack

Like breathing in opaque darkness
Stranded on the shoreline –
The entire sea composed of raging rip tides

Internalize *this* –
There is always something beautiful to come

Glistening light eases over me;
Wash me in Your love.

Hope is not hollow.

His Promise:
I. Am. Safe.

There is something about rumbling thunder
In the midst of a dream service.
God is in this place, in the midst of our hearts,
Desiring our desires and
Hoping along with us to make them come to pass.

Stars in your eyes
Awaken to a brand new light,
And this light, it brightens the night,
Not just in one place, but all around.

Your soul is a beautiful thing,
Beloved by the Greatest Lover of all loves
The King of kings
The Lord over all lords

Help me dream of You
And of all things we'll do.

His Spirit is majesty,
So your spirit is majestic.

If I could put into words the sunset of today:
Blue to white, like tiger stripes

His Promises for us,
They far outweigh the stars.

Darling, don't you know?
You are always in the right place when I am near
Come here, and you will belong

Compassion of the self,
My dear,
That's the grandest kind of all.

Rediscover wonder
Follow the river to a waterfall – and jump
Fall into beauty you never imagined was possible
Hold your breath tight as it envelops you in goodness

In the quiet of a sweet surrender,
Peace resounds across the hearts of all involved
In the silence of a sweet surrender,
We will find all the freedom we have lacked.

Jesus Christ, the Laughter Giver
He is the King of kings,
The Giver of laughter and joy.

Beware the cockroach thoughts
The nagging hatred that won't let you sleep

The girl who couldn't find the light
Has become the girl who runs straight to it.

It's not your house,
But it's a home

He sees your eyes wrinkle in joy
Every time you smile,
And He sees your heart sparkle
With a billion glimmers of hope.

You are royalty
Your soul was created with Creator's own image
And such beauty would never be less.

Forgiveness is a gift of healing
Not to those who hurt us
But to the hurt that lives inside our souls

We begin at the ending,
Following the trail least travelled
Forged by those who've gone before us

It is so easy to dwell in the valley of anger and hurt.
It is so easy to drop all else and zero in how I was wronged.
But through all of that,
I know I've been called to walk a greater path.
I know I've been called to peace.

We dress our own selves in guilt.
We must choose to be clothed in freedom.

Set a fire; let it burn

Never ending is His goodness.
Steadfast is His faithfulness.
Everlasting is His peace.
Forever, He remains.

In His mind, you were fathomed;
In His heart, you were loved.

You will find beauty in the clouds
Unreproducible sights no camera can capture,
And your heart will fall immeasurably in love
With something only God could create.

All the colors of the rainbow thrive individually,
But in this setting, they are unified
And will remain so until the end of the earth.

Dear Readers,

Thank you so much for joining me on this journey. I hope it has changed you the way it's changed me.

I mentioned *The Everglow* by Mae at the beginning of this book. The CD has always stuck with me for some reason, and now that I look back, I think it's because the form of it has, itself, formed the way I write. Open with the thing you want to change, and meander your way to changing it. By the end, you find yourself exactly where you wanted to be, and you've found some really beautiful places along the way.

A prayer for you:

May you find the strength to look for love where there seems to
   be none. I promise it is there.
May you find the courage to look for value when you've been
   told you have none. I promise it is there.
May you have the whimsy to find the beauty locked in every
   single moment. I promise it is there.
And to borrow a line from "May I Always," may you follow
   Him surely in every step, every way, even through a
   thousand different lands.

I love you.

With all sincerity in Christ,
Meg

Suicide hotline and contact info:

Meg Lynch: meglynch203@gmail.com
Facebook: message my page at www.facebook.com/
  meglynch203
Instagram: www.instagram.com/meglynch203

The US National Suicide Prevention Hotline: 1-800-273-8255;
  chat.suicidepreventionlifeline.org

TEEN Nineline Hotline: 1-800-999-9999; www.nineline.org

The Trevor Project: 1-866-488-7386; text: 1-202-304-1200;
  chat: available 7 seven days a week 3pm-9pm EST; http://
  www.thetrevorproject.org/pages/get-help-now

Good books to aid in healing:
Why Does He Do That? by Lundy Bancroft
Simply Tuesday by Emily P. Freeman